Who Was
Steve Irwin?

Who Was Steve Irwin?

by Dina Anastasio

illustrated by Jim Eldridge

Penguin Workshop

For Jason, Isabella, and Eliza—DA

PENGUIN WORKSHOP
An Imprint of Penguin Random House LLC, New York

Text copyright © 2015 by Dina Anastasio.
Illustrations copyright © 2015 by Penguin Random House LLC. All rights reserved.
Published by Penguin Workshop, an imprint of Penguin Random House LLC, New York.
PENGUIN and PENGUIN WORKSHOP are trademarks of Penguin Books Ltd.
WHO HQ & Design is a registered trademark of Penguin Random House LLC.
Printed in the USA.

Visit us online at www.penguinrandomhouse.com.

Library of Congress Control Number: 2015939757

ISBN 9780448488387   15 14

Contents

Contents

Who Was
Steve Irwin?

When Steve Irwin was a boy, he followed his father everywhere. He had so many questions, his dad thought Steve's mind might explode. Why is that snake hissing? How come that gecko's tail is missing? Do crocodiles cry crocodile tears?

Steve's father, Bob, was a reptile expert. He knew more about snakes and lizards and crocodiles than most other people in Australia. He had no trouble answering Steve's questions.

Snakes hiss to scare away predators, he'd say. Geckos shed their tails so they won't get caught. Crocodiles make tears to clean their eyes; they don't really cry.

When Steve was nine, his father took him to

the wilderness to catch his first crocodile. Steve's questions changed.

Steve: Why do you capture crocodiles?

Bob: To move them to safe places where people won't kill them.

Steve: Why do people kill them?

Bob: Because they're afraid.

Steve: Why are they afraid?

Bob: Because they don't understand them.

Steve Irwin never stopped asking questions. When he grew up, he searched for answers by himself. He found them everywhere. On the branches of a mango tree. Inside a kangaroo's pouch. Beside a riverbank.

Before long, Steve knew so much that a TV station asked him to share what he had learned. His show was called *The Crocodile Hunter.* Steve's audience grew, first in Australia, then all over the world. He took viewers along as he explored the wildlife he loved. He noticed everything. Every little snake was gorgeous. Every crocodile was

a little beauty. People started looking at wildlife differently. They were curious now. They weren't as afraid anymore.

Steve Irwin spent his life trying to protect wildlife. Like his father, he continued to teach others.

Steve never lost that excitement he felt when he was a child. "Crikey," he would whisper to the camera when he spotted another "gorgeous" creature. But he also never forgot what Bob had told him. "Careful, mate!" he would add. "Danger! Danger! Danger!"

Chapter 1
Snakes and Joeys

February 22, 1962, was a big day for Lyn Irwin. It was her twentieth birthday. It was also the day that her second child, and first son, was born. Stephen Robert Irwin was born in a small town called Upper Ferntree Gully, near Melbourne.

By the time Steve was a year old, he was scurrying toward the front door. There was so much to explore. As they hurried to catch him, Lyn and Bob Irwin knew they were in for a wild ride. Steve's older sister, Joy, knew it, too. She was old enough to understand that she'd better remember to close all doors everywhere or this new little brother of hers would be missing again.

To Steve, the world outside the house was a wonderland. Steve's father was a very successful plumber. But more than anything, Bob Irwin loved snakes and other reptiles. Steve was a curious child. He wanted to play with his father's snakes.

AUSTRALIA

AUSTRALIA IS THE ONLY COUNTRY IN THE WORLD THAT IS ALSO A CONTINENT. IT IS THE SMALLEST CONTINENT AND THE SIXTH-LARGEST COUNTRY. THIS ENGLISH-SPEAKING COUNTRY IS SURROUNDED BY WATER. THE PACIFIC OCEAN IS ON THE EAST. THE INDIAN OCEAN IS ON THE WEST. AUSTRALIA'S LARGEST CITIES ARE SYDNEY, MELBOURNE, BRISBANE, PERTH, AND ADELAIDE. THEY ARE ALL NEAR THE OCEAN. MUCH OF AUSTRALIA'S MIDDLE IS A DRY REMOTE DESERT AREA CALLED *THE OUTBACK.*

Snakes can be very dangerous, Bob would
say. Some snakes will not hurt you. But some
are poisonous—like the brown, tiger, and taipan
snakes that live in the woods.

EASTERN
BROWN
SNAKE

TIGER SNAKE

TAIPAN SNAKE

Poisonous snakes shoot venom out through
their fangs when they bite. Snakes don't like to be
disturbed. It scares them. So stay back!

The world inside Steve's house was also
interesting. Steve's mother was trained as a nurse.
She had cared for newborn babies. Lyn Irwin
loved babies. All kinds of babies. She loved them
as much as her husband loved snakes and lizards
and plants.

Sometimes Lyn and Steve would spot an injured kangaroo, koala, or opossum lying by the side of the road. Lyn would stop the car and take the animal home. She would also check to see if there was a baby in the mother's pouch. Baby kangaroos, koalas, wallabies, and opossums are called *joeys*. Steve's first playmates were joeys.

As Steve grew older, he obeyed his father's warnings about snakes and other dangerous animals. He stood back instead of trying to grab at the snakes. He watched how Bob gently handled the reptiles with love and respect.

When Bob went into the woods to look for
snakes and lizards, Steve came along. Bob pointed
out all kinds of wildlife. He explained how frogs
were disappearing because of water pollution.

They needed help, or soon they might become extinct. There would be no more of them. People were clearing the land and cutting down trees. Beautiful birds were also losing their homes.

When they went out to see the crocodiles, Steve moved close to the riverbank. These are

FRESHWATER CROCODILE

freshwater crocs, Bob would say. They live in rivers and creeks where the water is fresh, not salty. *Saltwater crocs* live in salty oceans. Sometimes they wander into freshwater. Salties are much bigger and much more dangerous than freshies.

SALTWATER CROCODILE

Bob never seemed frightened of the wildlife he loved. But sometimes he sounded angry. People wanted to kill these beautiful crocs and snakes and lizards. Poachers shot them and sold their skins to people who made shoes and handbags.

When Steve was six years old, his father gave him a twelve-foot python. Pythons do not produce venom, so they are not poisonous. Pythons kill their prey by squeezing. They can be dangerous, too. Bob taught Steve to be very careful.

Steve loved his new pet. He held it gently, like his mother had done when she cared for sick and injured baby animals.

In the evenings, Bob and Lyn talked about how they wished they could spend all their time caring for wildlife. There were three children now—Joy, Steve, and the new baby, Mandy.

The Irwins discussed buying some land near the ocean. They could work together as a family. Bob would be able to spend time with the reptiles. Lyn would have more room to care for baby animals. Together they could teach about Australian wildlife. They would create a park. People would pay to see the animals.

The more they talked, the more excited they became. They would live in a trailer while they built a house. Bob was good at building. He'd helped build houses before. Bob drew up plans for the house and the park. Lyn was in charge of money.

The year was 1970. Steve Irwin was eight years old. The Irwins came to a decision. Now was the time to follow their dream.

Chapter 2
Growing Up in a Zoo

Beerwah, Queensland, seemed like the perfect place to build a reptile park. Beerwah was in one of Australia's most beautiful areas—the Sunshine Coast. Tourists flocked to the area, especially in the summer.

The Pacific Ocean was a twenty-minute drive away. The Glass House Mountains were fifteen minutes to the south. People from all over the world came to hike there.

To the west and south were forests and rivers where snakes slithered and crocodiles basked in the sun. The city of Brisbane was an hour south.

The Irwins bought four acres of land, parked their small RV trailer, and tried to settle in. Living in a trailer was cramped, to say the least. Two adults, three kids, snakes and baby animals, and everything the family owned.

Bob went to work building a shed and some reptile enclosures. Soon, the Irwins' new life began to seem normal. The family belongings were in the shed. Many of the reptiles were in homes of their own. Bob and Lyn were beginning to live their dream. It would take time to build the perfect house, but no one seemed to mind. Living in the RV was fun. The RV would be their home for two years.

Every morning, Steve would dress in his
school uniform for Landsborough State School.
The school was not far from his new home,
but Steve was often late. Lyn was always ready.

Joy and Mandy were ready, too. Steve was ready,
but nobody could ever find him. While Lyn and
the girls waited in the car, Bob searched the woods
and called Steve's name. Where was Steve?

Out exploring! There was so much to discover
in this exciting new world. Trees filled with
laughing kookaburras and other birds. Streams
alive with fish and snakes.

By the end of 1970, the Beerwah Reptile Park was up and running. Lyn and Bob placed ads in the local paper. Reporters wrote newspaper articles. People came to the park and told their friends about it. Tourists arrived. More enclosures were built. The zoo was growing. At last, the Irwins were making money doing what they loved.

THE BUSH

AUSTRALIANS REFER TO AREAS AWAY FROM TOWNS AND CITIES AS *THE BUSH*. PEOPLE GO TO THE BUSH TO GET AWAY FROM CROWDS AND NOISE. THEY CAMP IN THE WOODS BENEATH MANGO TREES. THEY LISTEN TO BIRDS AND SEE FISH IN CLEAR WATER. BUT CITIES ARE GROWING LARGER. POLLUTION AND LAND CLEARING ARE PUSHING THE BUSH FARTHER AND FARTHER AWAY.

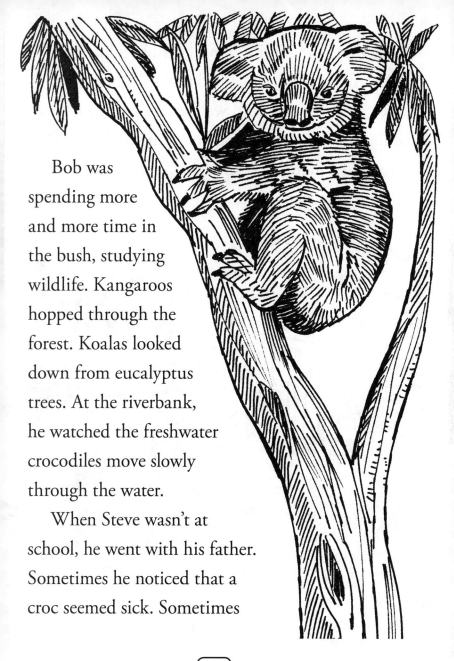

Bob was
spending more
and more time in
the bush, studying
wildlife. Kangaroos
hopped through the
forest. Koalas looked
down from eucalyptus
trees. At the riverbank,
he watched the freshwater
crocodiles move slowly
through the water.

When Steve wasn't at
school, he went with his father.
Sometimes he noticed that a
croc seemed sick. Sometimes

they thrashed angrily. Steve heard bulldozers in the distance. Bob explained that the noise upset the crocs. Nearby, land was being cleared for new buildings. The water was becoming polluted. The crocodiles' home was changing. That was why they were getting sick.

Bob and Steve wanted to rescue the crocs. Bob knew they were in danger of being killed. If land was being cleared, a golf course or home wasn't far behind. Bob knew that many people didn't want crocs nearby. They were afraid. Some people were shooting the crocs. But the crocs were afraid, too. Intruders were disturbing their homes.

Bob decided to move the crocs to new areas where the water was clean and they would be safe. But first he would have to find a way to care for the sick crocs. He would build a safe place in the park. Sick and injured crocs would stay until they were well enough to be returned to the wild.

As Steve watched from a distance, Bob used mesh netting to capture the crocs. Bob explained that crocs hated to be disturbed, but they calmed down if their eyes were covered. He taught Steve how to make a hood blindfold. He showed him how to tie up a croc's jaws so it couldn't bite.

Sometimes, when the croc was secure and wrapped in mesh, Steve helped his dad carry it to the truck for the trip back to the park.

Steve and Bob built larger enclosures for the crocs. They filled their ponds with clean, healthy water. After the crocs were well again, Bob and Steve returned many to the wild. But some remained in the park.

Bob loved telling people about the wildlife in his park. Before long, the word was out. Bob Irwin was well-known as an expert on snakes. Now he was talking about crocs, too.

CROC FACTS

CROCODILES AND ALLIGATORS ARE PREHISTORIC ANIMALS, LIKE DINOSAURS. DINOSAURS BECAME EXTINCT SIXTY-FIVE MILLION YEARS AGO, BUT SOMEHOW, CROCS AND GATORS SURVIVED.

CROCODILES ARE NOT THE SAME AS ALLIGATORS. CROCODILES LIVE MAINLY IN AFRICA, AUSTRALIA, INDIA, AND SOUTH AMERICA. MOST ALLIGATORS LIVE IN THE SOUTHERN UNITED STATES AND CHINA.

CROCODILES ARE GENERALLY LARGER THAN ALLIGATORS. SOME ARE TWENTY FEET LONG AND WEIGH TWO THOUSAND POUNDS.

CROCODILES HAVE POINTED, V-SHAPED SNOUTS.

CROCODILE

ALLIGATORS HAVE ROUNDED, U-SHAPED SNOUTS.

CROCODILES ALWAYS SHOW SOME OF THEIR BOTTOM TEETH. AN ALLIGATOR'S BOTTOM TEETH CANNOT BE SEEN WHEN ITS MOUTH IS CLOSED.

CROCODILES SWEAT THROUGH THEIR MOUTHS. THAT'S WHY THEIR MOUTHS ARE OPEN SO MUCH OF THE TIME.

SALTWATER CROCS ARE SOMETIMES CALLED *SALTIES*.

FRESHWATER CROCS ARE CALLED *FRESHIES*. FRESHIES ARE SMALLER THAN SALTIES.

ALLIGATOR

Chapter 3
Catching Crocs

One day, when Steve was nine, Bob heard that land was being cleared to the north. Dams were being built. The fish and reptiles that lived in the river were disturbed by the explosions. The crocodiles were frightening the workers.

Bob knew there was a chance the crocs would be shot. He decided to head up the river and see what he could do.

Steve wanted to go. But there was this problem called school. Nevertheless, Steve had made up his mind. He was going with his father, and that was that! "If it looked like I wasn't going to go on a field trip, I'd roll around on the ground and wave me arms in the air," he said later.

Bob enjoyed having Steve with him. But he had a problem, too. Crocs can be dangerous. Especially saltwater crocs. Bob made a decision. Steve wasn't going anywhere until they had a good long talk.

Saltwater crocodiles are known as killing machines. They will eat anything—horses, cows, wild pigs, and small, or overly excited boys who aren't being careful. Freshwater crocs eat fish and insects most of the time. Freshies aren't usually interested in humans, but they will bite when they're upset.

A croc's hearing is very sensitive. Loud noises, like explosions, bulldozers, and noisy boys, terrify them. Crocs don't know when people are trying to save their lives. They'll thrash and fight if someone tries to trap them.

Bob had always taught Steve to be calm and silent around crocs. But it was hard for Steve. He could barely sit still.

When Bob said he could come along, Steve jumped up and down and raced around the house.

Maybe Bob would let him catch a freshie and wrap it up. He'd watched his father do it enough times.

The next day, Bob and Steve packed up their truck and headed north toward the river. Steve begged to catch a croc. This time, Bob agreed.

Catching crocs is best done at night. When the river is dark, a croc's eyes gleam bright, like a shiny red reflective road sign. Bob and Steve waited.

Finally, it was time. Steve climbed into the front of their dinghy. Bob sat in the back. Holding their flashlights, they drifted slowly through the murky water.

"There's one," Steve gasped. Bob and Steve peered into the water and studied the croc's head. It was small. A small head meant Steve could catch it. The croc was probably no more than five feet long. Bigger than that was too dangerous for a nine-year-old.

The croc was definitely a freshie. I can catch this little beauty, Steve told Bob. He put his flashlight down and leaned over.

A moment later, Steve flew off the boat and scrambled onto the croc's back. Its tail was thrashing. Even so, Steve managed to trap it between his legs and hang on tight.

The croc wasn't as small as Steve had thought. This little beauty was as big as Steve. As the croc struggled to get free, Bob tossed his light aside

and reached out. One arm grabbed Steve. The other snatched up the croc. They landed in the boat together, croc and boy. The blindfold and ropes came out. The jaws were secured.

Later, as they moved the croc to a safer part of the river, away from the explosions, Steve felt good. He had done it. He had captured his first crocodile. He had relocated it. It had been exciting and fun. The croc was safe now. People would not hurt it. On that day, Steve Irwin knew that no matter what happened, he was going to spend his life saving these amazing reptiles.

AUSTRALIAN WILDLIFE

PLATYPUS: A MIXED-UP MAMMAL. IT HAS A DUCK'S BILL AND WEBBED FEET, A BEAVER'S TAIL, AND AN OTTER'S BODY. MALES SHOOT VENOM OUT OF THEIR HEELS.

DINGO: A WILD DOG THAT SOMETIMES TRAVELS IN PACKS.

KOALA: CUTE LITTLE ANIMALS THAT ENJOY HANGING OUT IN EUCALYPTUS TREES. THEY ARE NOT BEARS. KOALAS CARRY BABIES IN THEIR POUCHES, AND ARE THEREFORE *MARSUPIAL* MAMMALS.

LAUGHING KOOKABURRA: A KINGFISHER BIRD. THEY MAKE LOUD, LAUGHING BIRDCALLS.

NUMBAT: A BANDED ANTEATER.

TASMANIAN DEVIL: AN ANGRY, TEETH-BARING MARSUPIAL. ALMOST ALL NOW LIVE ON THE ISLAND

OF TASMANIA, SOUTH OF AUSTRALIA.

WALLABY: SIMILAR TO BUT SMALLER THAN THEIR AUSTRALIAN KANGAROO COUSINS.

WOMBAT: ANOTHER POUCHED MARSUPIAL. THEY ARE NOCTURNAL AND SPEND THEIR NIGHTS DIGGING BURROWS AND EATING GRASS AND BARK.

Chapter 4
Surfing with Salties

As Steve grew older, Bob began to depend on him to help save troubled freshies, snakes, and lizards. Sometimes they stayed in the bush for days, sleeping under the stars, tracking and capturing problem crocs. As Steve grew, so did the crocs he was allowed to capture.

Steve was different than most of the kids in his school. While he was out catching crocs, other boys were playing rugby, soccer, and cricket. At Steve's home, there were lizards and crocs to feed and snakes to play with. As the park expanded, there were bigger and better enclosures to help build. Lyn needed help with the baby opossums, koalas, kangaroos, birds, and lizards. *Why would anyone want to play sports*

after school when they could be doing this? Steve
asked himself.

But there was one sport he loved almost as much as he loved catching crocs—surfing. By the time he was in high school, Steve was a great surfer. Steve attended Caloundra State High School. The school was about a half hour from his house. But it was a short five-minute drive from one of the best surfing beaches. Steve began to spend more and more time surfing.

By the time Steve finished high school in 1979, the Beerwah Reptile Park was overflowing with all kinds of wildlife. Poisonous and nonpoisonous snakes wrapped around tree branches. Lizards and chameleons skittered past Lyn's kangaroos, koalas, and baby birds. There was so much to do. When he was home, Steve helped his sisters collect money from the people who came to see the reptiles. He showed the visitors how he fed the crocodiles and other reptiles. He tried to answer their questions.

As for Bob Irwin, he was becoming well-known. Articles about his talks at the park were printed in newspapers all over the area.

Bob believed that education was the best way to help people understand the wildlife he loved. Once they came to know crocodiles and snakes, they wouldn't fear them. They wouldn't shoot them. In time, people from all over the world came to hear Bob talk. The money the visitors paid was put back into the park.

In 1982, the Irwins bought four acres next to the park. Bob and Steve worked the land together.

They dug holes. They put up fences. Now the crocs and other wildlife had more room to wander safely.

The park was overflowing with all kinds of Australian wildlife. Newspapers called it one of the area's best places to visit.

In 1980 the Beerwah Reptile Park became the Queensland Reptile and Fauna Park. Steve was twenty years old. He had been working at home with his parents. Now, he was itching to get back to the bush. There were crocs in trouble that needed to be relocated.

Bob was ready, too. Visitors to the park had been asking him about the dangerous saltwater crocs that had moved into rivers and creeks up north.

I read that they eat people, the visitors said. They're gigantic! I'm afraid to go near the water. They should be shot!

Bob tried to explain that these creatures had been around for more than one hundred million years. Longer than the dinosaurs. Somehow, they had managed to survive. Until now. People want to wear crocodile shoes, he said. They want to carry crocodile purses. So they shoot these magnificent reptiles for their skins. If something isn't done, salties will become extinct.

The Australian government had placed saltwater crocodiles on the endangered species list. Killing crocs meant heavy fines, or even prison. But salties were still being shot.

Until now, Steve had spent most of his time trying to save and relocate freshwater crocs. Now he wanted to find a way to save salties.

In 1985, Steve heard that the government was setting up the East Coast Crocodile Management Program to control the saltie problem. Steve and Bob signed on as volunteers. From then on, they would spend their time capturing and relocating "nuisance" Australian saltwater crocodiles. The salties they couldn't relocate would be brought back to the park.

Chapter 5
Wildlife Warrior

In 1985, Steve Irwin met a boy who would become his best mate for the rest of his life. Steve was home from the bush, helping out at the park, when Wes Mannion stopped by with his family. Wes was fourteen. He was eight years younger than Steve, but that didn't matter to either of them. Snakes mattered. Crocs mattered. Opossum joeys mattered.

WES MANNION

Just like Steve, Wes loved animals and wanted to learn. He asked Bob if he could help out after school and on weekends.

The park was bigger now. There was plenty to do. Wes was ready for any kind of work. Cleaning, building, caring for the animals. Anything—as long as he could be around wildlife.

It wasn't long before Wes was spending almost all his time at the park. Whenever he could, he'd stop what he was doing and join the crowd for one of Bob's talks. Before long, Wes was a member of the family. Visitors thought he was Steve's little brother. That was just fine with Steve.

Now it was the three of them—Bob, Steve, and "little brother" Wes—catching freshies. This time, Wes sat in the front of the dinghy, holding the flashlight, looking at head size. Then, finally, he leaped into the dark water and trapped his first croc. Sometimes Wes also went along when Steve and Bob were going to relocate salties.

In 1987, Bob decided they needed more room
in the park for saltwater crocodiles that couldn't
be relocated. Every day, he heard of another saltie
in danger of being killed. He would build a large
area in the park to house these salties. Everybody
went to work. Before long the Crocodile
Environmental Park was ready.

Wes stayed behind to help with the new salties that Steve brought home. By 1988, Wes was working at the park full-time.

Steve loved going up north with Bob. But the park was growing fast, and Bob was needed at home. Steve decided to stay up in the bush. He loved camping alone beside the rivers and creeks. He loved it all. Locating a rogue saltie. Building a net trap. Wrestling a huge, angry croc into a dinghy. Hoisting it into his truck and into a crate. Moving it to a safer place. Saving its life.

It was awesome. At home, he'd try to explain his experiences, but nobody could really understand. Nobody but Bob and Wes.

Bob decided Steve needed a video camera. Steve began talking to the camera like he was telling a friend all about his life in the wild. Sometimes his little sister, Mandy, came along and became his camerawoman.

Crikey, he'd whisper as he wrapped the jaws of a thrashing saltie.

What a little beauty! he'd say, pointing the camera at a burrowing wombat.

Danger! Danger! Danger! he'd cry as an eastern brown snake happened by.

Steve started thinking about teaching, like Bob. There was so much information to share about all the Australian wildlife he saw in the bush. Dingoes and wild pigs and salties and wallabies.

DINGO

Sometimes at night, when the mosquitos were bad or the rain was pounding outside his tent, he'd think it might be nice to have a friend. Someone to talk to about all the fantastic things he'd learned that day.

WALLABY

Maybe he could get a dog.

Steve first heard about Sui on December 25, 1988. It was Christmas Day. A new Staffordshire

bull terrier had just been born. Steve decided this was the dog he wanted. He would name her Sui.

They would go up into the bush together and sleep under the stars. But first, there were a few things Sui would have to learn—like how to avoid snakes, how to stay back when Steve was busy with a hungry croc, how to avoid being eaten when chasing a wild pig, and how to keep very, very quiet.

Sui arrived at the park six weeks later. Steve started training her right away. When she was ready, Steve led her to the truck. Sui hopped in the front seat and looked up at Steve. That night, they slept in Steve's sleeping bag together. The next evening, they searched for a rogue saltie. Sui was worried when Steve jumped into the river and crept up behind the enormous croc. But she stayed in the boat. She didn't bark.

Soon, Sui was helping Steve confuse the crocs. When Steve was about to capture a croc, he would throw a stick. Sui was a great swimmer, and she would race for it. The croc would watch Sui swim

toward the stick. That would give Steve time to blindfold the croc and secure its jaws.

Sui loved helping Steve. Every time she saw Steve with his sleeping bag, she'd hop in the front seat of the truck and bark. Soon they would be off. Together. Sui and her best pal, Steve.

Steve thought he'd stay in the bush forever—until he met a man who changed his life.

IRWIN'S TURTLE

ONE DAY IN THE EARLY 1990S, STEVE AND
BOB WERE FISHING IN A RIVER WITH SUI. THEY
NOTICED A SNAPPING TURTLE WITH A WHITE HEAD
AND A PINK NOSE SWIMMING NEARBY. STEVE AND
BOB MOVED CLOSER AND EXAMINED THE TURTLE.
NO ONE HAD EVER SEEN A TURTLE LIKE THIS
ONE. THE TURTLE WAS NAMED *ELSEYA IRWINI*, OR
IRWIN'S SNAPPING TURTLE.

Chapter 6
The Crocodile Hunter

JOHN STAINTON

John Stainton was a filmmaker. One day he stopped by to make a TV commercial in the Irwins' park. He was filming the animals. Steve was home for a visit. He was showing visitors how they fed the crocs.

John was amazed. When the show was over, John and Steve talked for a long time. John asked what it was like catching crocs. Steve gave him some of the films he'd shot in the bush.

John put the films away and made his commercial. When he took them out again, he couldn't believe what he was seeing. The croc was terrifying to John. But Steve didn't seem at all afraid.

Crikey, Steve was saying, this little beauty sure is hungry. John couldn't believe how excited Steve was about the croc. This guy *really* thought a croc was the most beautiful thing he'd ever seen! He was waving his arms around and making all kinds of strange animal sounds.

Gorgeous was one of Steve's favorite words.

Everything seemed gorgeous to him. The croc's razor-sharp, glistening teeth were *gorgeous*. Its lashing tail was *gorgeous*.

Steve Irwin's life seemed to be one great big gorgeous adventure.

John watched the raw videos over and over. An idea was bubbling in his brain. He called Steve. Would Steve mind if he showed the films to Australia's Channel Ten network?

Crikey! Steve said.

The producers at Channel Ten were as amazed by the films as John had been. They loved the way Steve looked right into the camera when he explained things. They loved how excited he got when he talked to the animals. They all saw what a great teacher this guy was.

It's time to get to work, John told Steve. The producers want ten one-hour episodes. They want it just like the ones you filmed with your own camera. Up close and personal.

But Steve had other things to think about. He had taken over the park the year before, and it was more popular than ever. He had been adding more land and more animals. His parents, Bob and Lyn, had retired to Rosedale, a small town farther north. But most important of all—Steve had met the perfect woman.

Terri Raines visited the park in October 1991. She was there to check out the wildlife. Terri lived in America, in Eugene, Oregon, and was touring Australia to learn about the animals that lived there.

TERRI RAINES

Steve was showing visitors how the crocs in the park were fed. Terri was fascinated. Steve and Terri came from different worlds. Yet as they talked, they realized their backgrounds were very similar. Like Lyn Irwin, Terri's father couldn't pass by an injured animal on the side of the road. Like Lyn, he'd care for them at home. When they were better, he'd release them into the wild. Terri loved animals as much as her father did. When she grew up, she started a clinic called Cougar Country that cared for injured wild bobcats and other animals.

Steve and Terri talked so much that Sui began to bark and whine. Steve and Terri knew she was jealous and tried to comfort her, but Sui wasn't having it—at least at first.

Terri left Australia shortly after meeting Steve. But she returned four months later. Soon, Terri and Steve were talking about getting married. On June 4, 1992, Steve married Terri in Eugene, Oregon.

Then it was back to work.

Steve was anxious to get started on the TV show. John was making plans. Everyone wanted Terri to be in it. It would be Steve and Terri. Terri and Steve. Terri wondered what she was getting into, but she was ready for anything. It was all so exciting. They'd be spending time in the bush. She'd learn about poisonous snakes. She'd help Steve capture a croc. They'd take Sui along. Sui and Terri were friends now. A honeymoon for the Irwins would have to wait.

Chapter 7
Fame and Fortune

Australia's Channel Ten began showing the ten episodes in 1992. They called the program *The Crocodile Hunter.* Five years later, in 1997, the Animal Planet network aired the first episode in the United States.

It wasn't long before *The Crocodile Hunter* was being watched all around the world. Eventually, the audience would rise to five hundred million viewers in more than one hundred countries.

Steve and Terri were famous. Steve wasn't sure how he felt about that. He had never been interested in fame. Sometimes he missed his privacy. All Steve had ever wanted was to help people understand the wildlife he loved. But there were good things about fame. He could learn and teach as he traveled the world in search of exciting new wildlife. He could introduce viewers to endangered species. He could help them understand why caring for wildlife was so important.

Maybe he could take them to one of the tiny Komodo National Park islands in Indonesia. He could introduce viewers to the largest, most dangerous lizards in the world. Komodo dragons are huge. Many grow to be almost ten feet long.

Komodo dragons look like dinosaurs but are actually lizards. They will eat almost anything. They have lurked around Indonesia for millions of years.

Steve arranged to travel to Komodo National Park to shoot an episode of *The Crocodile Hunter*. As the boat approached, a Komodo dragon on the dock greeted the team.

Visitors to the park must travel around with park rangers for their own safety. But Steve and his crew were allowed to roam and film on their own. Gigantic Komodo dragons were everywhere. Strutting. Nipping. Whipping their tails at Steve. Strolling through the mangroves. Hunting for wild pigs.

A Komodo dragon with a fishhook in his throat thought Steve was dinner as he tried to remove it. "Danger, danger, danger," Steve announced as he scrambled up a tree. The lizard tried to get to him, but Steve escaped.

Another dragon was swimming toward a nearby island in search of goats. "Commotion in the ocean!" Steve said.

The episode, "Steve and the Dragon," aired on the Animal Planet network in 1999.

As Steve's reputation grew, it seemed like more and more people needed him. One day a call came in from Florida. The United States Air Force had a problem. Could Steve help?

Eglin Air Force Base is in northern Florida. The training ground was crawling with rattlesnakes. How could rangers practice parachuting when the place was filled with pygmy rattlers, water moccasins, and

PYGMY RATTLESNAKE

other dangerous snakes? The officers had heard that Steve Irwin knew more about snakes

WATER MOCCASIN

than almost anyone.

Steve couldn't wait to go. There were so many things that excited him about visiting Florida. He could tell the rangers and viewers all the things he'd learned from Bob. How to tell the difference between poisonous and nonpoisonous snakes. How to spot them before they spot you. Why the

venom in a rattlesnake's fangs
might kill you. How to keep
yourself, and the snakes,
safe. Maybe he would
spot some of Florida's
gorgeous endangered
species, like the tiny,
silent burrowing
owl and the gopher
tortoise.

The rangers didn't just have to worry about snakes. They'd had to deal with alligators, too. Steve would teach them how to capture and move the gators to a safe place outside of the training area.

Steve and the rangers worked hard to move the dangerous snakes. The rangers were careful to protect the habitat. Finally, the rattlers and alligators had been moved. It was time to go home.

Steve was excited to get back to the zoo. Steve and Terri's family was growing. Their first child had been born on July 24, 1998. Her name was Bindi Sue Irwin. *Bindi* after one of Steve's favorite crocodiles. *Sue* after Sui, his favorite dog.

SOME OF STEVE'S FAVORITE AUSTRALIAN WORDS

CRIKEY! = WOW!

G'DAY = HELLO (SHORT FOR "GOOD DAY")

MATE = FRIEND

SWAG = BEDROLL

BLOKE = MAN

THE BUSH = OUTSIDE OF TOWN

NEVER NEVER = THE OUTBACK

CHOCKABLOCK = CROWDED OR FILLED WITH LOTS OF STUFF

DOWN UNDER = AUSTRALIA AND NEW ZEALAND

GOBSMACKED = SURPRISED

ROO = KANGAROO

JOEY = BABY KANGAROO, KOALA, WALLABY, OPOSSUM, WOMBAT

BOOMER = A LARGE MALE KANGAROO

MOB = HERD OF KANGAROOS

LOB IN = STOP BY FOR A VISIT

YOU LITTLE RIPPER = GORGEOUS, DELIGHTFUL

UTE = A PICKUP TRUCK

Chapter 8
Diary of a Zoo

Life at the zoo was busier than ever. *The Crocodile Hunter* series had made Steve and Terri very, very famous. Viewers in America, England, and other countries wanted to visit the zoo. They wanted to meet Harriet, the 170-year-old tortoise.

They wanted to watch the staff feed some of the most famous saltwater crocs—Agro, Graham, and the oldest croc, Acco. They knew Steve's daughter, Bindi, had been named after a croc. They wanted to meet this supercroc.

The Animal Planet network had an idea. They would film a new show about life at the zoo. Fans of Steve and Terri could meet the family and the animals.

The *Crocodile Hunter Diaries* began filming in 1998. It was shown on Animal Planet from 2002 to 2004. Now viewers on the other side of the world could watch Wes and Terri move loggerhead turtles back into the wild. They could see a python shed its skin.

The Australia Zoo staff all wore khaki shorts
and shirts, just like Steve. Viewers at home got
to know them. They watched the vets care for
sick kangaroos. They learned about magpies and
red foxes. They met a two-headed snake. They
followed Bindi as she helped operate on a hawk.

Steve was always busy. There were crocs to feed
and other animals to attend to. He talked to his
parents often. He called for advice when there was

a problem at the zoo. Bob and Lyn were always available to help out. But then, in February 2000, Steve got a terrible call. His mother, Lyn Irwin, had been killed in a car accident. It was a terrible time for the Irwin family.

But by 2003, there was good news. Terri was going to have another baby. The Irwins welcomed Robert Clarence Irwin on December 1, 2003. He was named after Steve's dad, Bob, and Terri's dad, Clarence. Now Bindi had a little brother. Viewers all over the world were able to meet him.

Calls continued to come in from far-off places:
Please come. We need help.

Steve and Terri couldn't wait to get back on the
road. It wasn't long before the whole family was
driving out to the bush or flying to America or
faraway islands.

Maewo   Vanuatu

South
Pacific
Ocean

Maewo is a tiny island in the South Pacific
Ocean. It is one of eighty-three islands in
the country of Vanuatu. When the Vanuatu
government called, Steve didn't hesitate.

A huge saltie was terrifying the island people of Maewo, one of the most beautiful islands in the South Pacific. The croc was twelve feet long and about 660 pounds. It was eating their pets. Fishermen were afraid to go out into the sea. Children no longer played on the beaches.

Steve and his team arrived in Maewo in early 2003. The staff of Vanuatu's Environment Unit thought the croc came from an island called Vanua Lava, far to the north. A powerful hurricane must have blown the supercroc away from its home.

Steve understood the problem. The people of Maewo needed to be protected. But this creature was an endangered species. Everyone wanted to save it. No one wanted it to be hurt.

This saltie needed help to find its way home. First, Steve and the crew would have to capture it. But how? *Crikey!* Steve thought. This wasn't going to be easy.

Steve and his crew built a strong floating trap

out of lightweight aluminum. The trap was lowered to the bottom of the ocean and attached to a pier post. Bait was placed in the trap. When the croc swam in, the trap gate closed. Then Steve pulled the croc onto the beach and trapped it between his legs. The islanders jumped back. Steve secured the croc's jaws and wrapped it in a net. The islanders moved closer. They peered down at the croc. They touched it. They were

beginning to understand this croc they feared. They weren't as scared anymore.

Steve was happy the *Crocodile Hunter Diaries* camera crew was filming. Viewers would see how important it was to find ways for humans and wildlife to share the planet.

A plane took the croc back to its home. Steve and his crew released it in the perfect environment—far from the villages. The island people cheered. Their old friend was back where it belonged, and they were safe.

Chapter 9
A Terrible Accident

In 2005, the Discovery Kids channel wanted Bindi to have her own show. Like Steve, she had grown up in a zoo. She knew almost as much about animals as Steve did.

Bindi wanted to do it. She was excited to teach kids to love animals. Steve and Terri agreed.

Bindi: The Jungle Girl began filming in 2006. Bindi was eight years old. On the show, she lived in a jungle tree house filled with snakes and birds and all kinds of Australian animals. Sometimes Steve and Terri came to visit. Sometimes her little brother, Robert, joined her.

Bindi and Steve took viewers to the United States to meet some American animals. They went to Africa to learn about lions. When they weren't traveling, Bindi explored the zoo. Wes was the manager now. He became part of the show, too. Bindi introduced the zoo animals. She pointed out all the gorgeous changes that were taking place. Viewers watched hundreds of birds in the rain forest aviary. They attended croc shows in the new 5,500-seat Crocoseum. They learned about crocodiles, birds, snakes, and other animals. They visited Steve's beloved new Wildlife Hospital, built in honor of his mother, Lyn. Bindi explained that volunteer wildlife

ambulances pick up injured or orphaned wildlife.
Vets at the hospital work to save them all.

WILDLIFE WARRIORS

IN 2002, STEVE AND TERRI STARTED A GROUP CALLED WILDLIFE WARRIORS TO HELP PEOPLE AROUND THE WORLD FIND WAYS TO RESCUE WILDLIFE. WILDLIFE WARRIORS HELP SAVE ANIMALS DURING HURRICANES, TSUNAMIS, EARTHQUAKES, AND OTHER NATURAL DISASTERS. LIKE STEVE, WARRIORS WEAR KHAKI. KHAKI CLOTHES HELP SHOW THEY ARE WORKING TOGETHER TO SAVE WILDLIFE AND THEIR HABITATS. WILDLIFE WARRIORS EDUCATE PEOPLE ALL OVER THE GLOBE. THEY RAISE MONEY TO BUY AND PRESERVE LAND FOR THE ANIMALS THEY LOVE.

When Steve wasn't helping Bindi, he was working on a new TV documentary. *Ocean's Deadliest* starred Steve and Philippe Cousteau Jr. Steve and Philippe introduced viewers to the great white shark, the blue-ringed octopus, the box

PHILIPPE COUSTEAU JR.

jellyfish, and other dangerous creatures in the South Pacific Ocean.

On September 4, 2006, Steve and Philippe were filming on Steve's boat around Australia's Great Barrier Reef. The weather turned too dark to film in deep water. Steve decided to do some shallow-water filming.

Steve got into a blow-up dinghy. Justin Lyons,

one of the cameramen, went with him. Near the shore, they noticed a huge, eight-foot-wide stingray fish. They decided to film it.

Stingrays are usually very calm creatures. But if a ray feels threatened, it will attack with the stinger on its tail. Some massive stingrays have stingers up to fourteen inches long.

Steve and Justin got into the water. Steve was behind the stingray. Justin was filming from the front. Suddenly the ray raised its tail and started stabbing at Steve with its stinger. One of the strikes pierced Steve's heart. At first, Justin didn't realize how badly hurt Steve was. He placed him in the dinghy and raced for help. But there was nothing anyone could do. Steve Irwin died quickly. He was forty-four years old.

The next day, newspapers all over the world announced that the Crocodile Hunter had died. Fans everywhere mourned their hero. People in Australia lowered flags in his honor. Australian officials suggested they hold a state funeral. The Irwin family talked it over and politely declined. Steve would want to be remembered as an "ordinary bloke," his father, Bob, said. Instead, a memorial service was held in the Australia Zoo's Crocoseum. All 5,500 seats were filled.

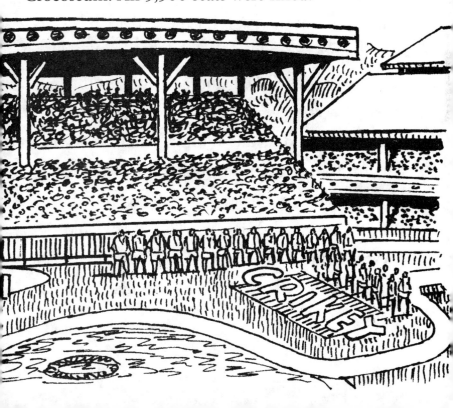

Chapter 10
Remembering Steve

Steve Irwin devoted his life to protecting the natural world and wildlife. His TV shows helped people understand why preserving an animal's habitat was so important. Steve and Terri used the money to buy large areas of land throughout Australia. But there was one place that Steve loved more than almost any other—the Wenlock River wetlands. Rare plants and animals thrive there. It was Steve's dream to protect this wild area from building and mining. After his death, the Australian government announced that 334,000 acres of the land Steve loved would be forever protected. Miners and builders would never disturb it. The Steve Irwin Wildlife Reserve would be looked after by the Australia Zoo.

Steve Irwin's work continues to be honored.

In 2007, the government of Rwanda in Africa named a baby mountain gorilla in honor of Steve.

In 2009, the Queensland Museum named a rare species of tree snail after Steve. The snail is called the *Crikey steveirwini*. The snail's yellow, orange, and brown bands reminded scientists of Steve's khaki uniform.

Each year, on

November 15, Wildlife Warriors all over the world celebrate Steve Irwin Day.

Terri, Bindi, and Robert are continuing Steve's work. At the zoo, they help care for the animals. They share their passion for wildlife with visitors. In 2012, Bindi and Robert filmed a twenty-four-episode Internet show. *Growing Up Wild* helped kids around the world understand the danger and beauty of wild animals.

Steve's memory lives on in the zoo he created
and the wildlife he protected. No one will ever
forget his passion, his dedication, and his message.
Wild animals are gorgeous, he said. Respect them.
It's their planet, too.

TIMELINE OF
STEVE IRWIN'S LIFE

1962 — Steve is born in Upper Ferntree Gully, Australia, on February 22

1970 — The Irwin family moves to Beerwah and opens the Beerwah Reptile Park

1979 — Steve graduates from Caloundra State High School

1980 — Beerwah Reptile Park is renamed Queensland Reptile and Fauna Park

1985 — Steve meets his best mate, Wes Mannion

1988 — Steve's dog, Sui, is born on Christmas Day

1992 — Steve marries Terri Raines on June 4 in Eugene, Oregon

1997-2004 — *The Crocodile Hunter* is shown on Animal Planet

1998 — Queensland Reptile and Fauna Park is renamed Australia Zoo
Steve's daughter, Bindi Sue, is born on July 24

1999-2001 — *The Crocodile Hunter's Croc Files* is shown on Animal Planet

2000 — Death of Steve's mother, Lyn

2002-2004 — *The Crocodile Hunter Diaries* is shown on Animal Planet

2003 — Steve's son, Robert Clarence Irwin, is born on December 1

2006 — Steve Irwin dies on the Great Barrier Reef on September 4

2007-2008 — *Bindi: The Jungle Girl* is shown on the Discovery Kids channel

2007 — *Ocean's Deadliest* is shown on the Animal Planet and Discovery channels on January 21

TIMELINE OF THE WORLD

US president John F. Kennedy is killed in Dallas, Texas, on November 22 — **1963**

Apollo 11 lands on the moon in July — **1969**
Sesame Street premieres on TV

Microsoft is founded — **1975**

Pac-Man video game is released in Japan — **1980**

MTV starts broadcasting rock-music videos — **1981**

E.T.: The Extra-Terrestrial comes out in movie theaters — **1982**

The wreckage of the *Titanic* is discovered — **1985**

The Soviet Union collapses — **1991**
The World Wide Web is created

Dolly the sheep is the first successfully cloned mammal — **1996**

The Supreme Court decides George W. Bush has won — **2000**
the presidential election against Al Gore

Terrorists attack the Twin Towers in New York City and — **2001**
the Pentagon in Washington, DC

Facebook is launched — **2004**

Hannah Montana, starring Miley Cyrus, debuts on TV — **2006**

Barack Obama becomes the first African American — **2009**
US president in January

BIBLIOGRAPHY

Baker, Trevor. **Steve Irwin: The Incredible Life of the Crocodile Hunter.** New York: Thunder's Mouth Press, 2006.

Crocodile Hunter, The. "Steve: Biography." http://www.crocodilehunter.com.au/crocodile_hunter/about_steve_terri/steve_biography.html.

* Irwin, Bindi, and Chris Kunz. **Croc Capers.** Bindi Wildlife Adventures 7. Naperville, IL: Sourcebooks Jabberwocky, 2012.

Irwin, Terri. **Steve & Me**. New York: Gallery Books, 2008.

National Geographic. "Australia." http://travel.nationalgeographic.com/travel/countries/australia-guide/.

National Geographic. "Saltwater Crocodile." http://animals.nationalgeographic.com/animals/reptiles/saltwater-crocodile.html.

O'Neil, Mike. "Irwin Family plays host to a reptilian brood." **Sunshine Coast Weekly**. July 9, 1986.

Outback Australia Travel Guide. "Australian Saltwater Crocodiles." http://www.outback-australia-travel-secrets. com/saltwater-crocodiles.html.

Robson, Frank. "Crikey, it's raw Stevo!" **Sydney Morning Herald.** September 4, 2006. http://www.smh.com.au/artic les/2006/09/04/1157222053963.html.

University of Bristol. "What are the major differences between crocodiles and alligators?" http://palaeo.gly.bris.ac.uk/palaeofiles/fossilgroups/ crocodylomorpha/Characters.html.

* Books for young readers

WEBSITES

Australia Zoo Official Website
http://www.australiazoo.com.au
http://www.australiazoo.com.au/about-us/the-irwins/